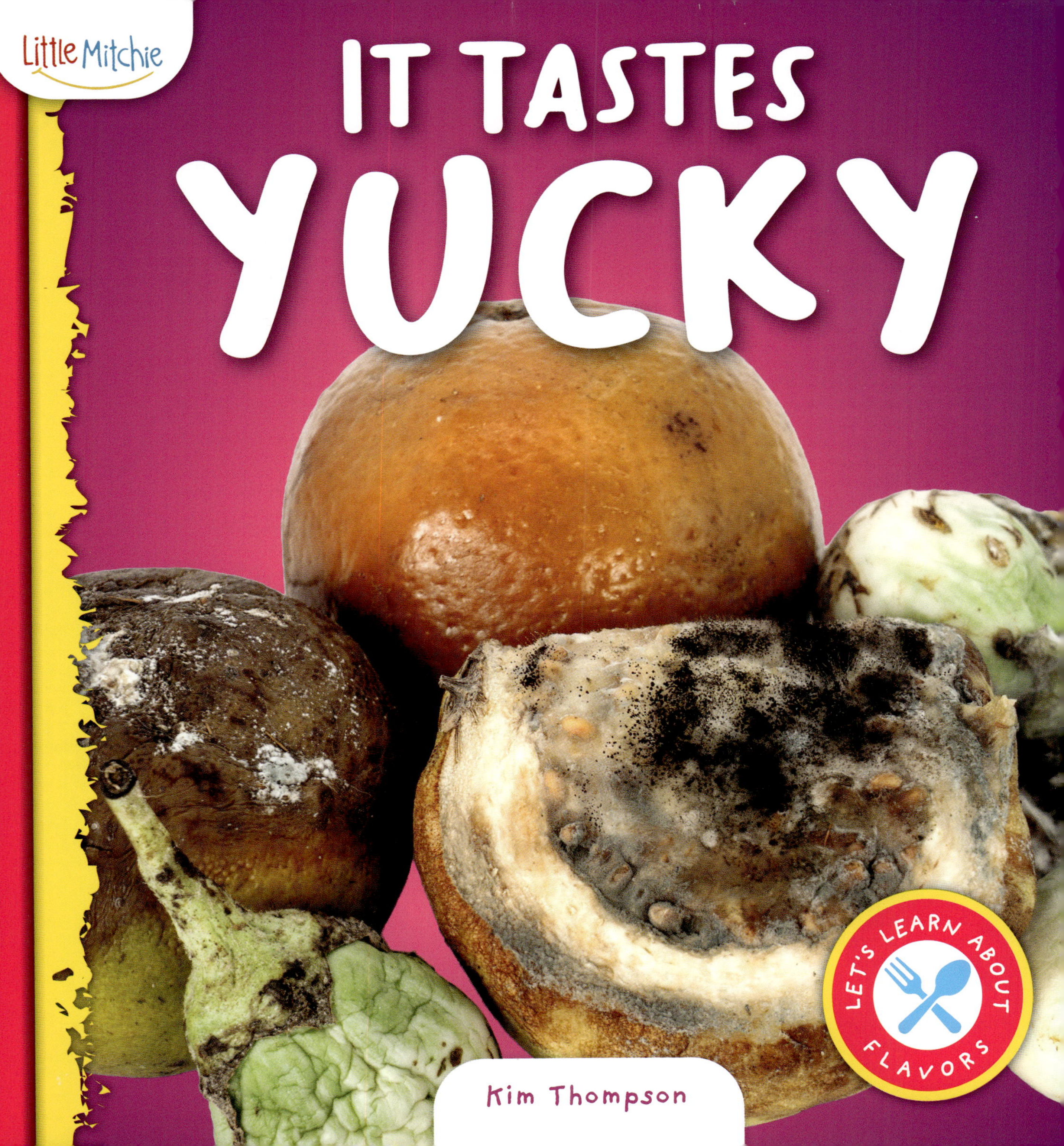
Little Mitchie
IT TASTES
YUCKY
LET'S LEARN ABOUT FLAVORS
Kim Thompson

## CREATING YOUNG NONFICTION READERS

*Little Mitchie* books spark curiosity and support early nonfiction reading for students in Grades 2-3. Designed to build vocabulary, support second language learners, and prepare readers for middle-grade content, each book includes helpful tips for parents and educators to build confidence and deepen understanding of the world.

## TIPS FOR READING NONFICTION WITH BEGINNING READERS

### Talk about Nonfiction

Begin by explaining that nonfiction books give us information that is true. The book will be organized around a specific topic or idea, and we may learn new facts through reading.

### Look at the Parts

Most nonfiction books have helpful features. Our *Little Mitchie* titles include color photographs and graphic aids, a table of contents, a glossary, and an index. Share the purpose of these features with your reader.

### Color Photos and Graphic Aids

A lot of information can be found by "reading" photos, charts, maps, and other graphic aids found within nonfiction texts. Help your reader learn more about the different ways information can be displayed.

### Table of Contents

Located at the front of the book, this list shows the big ideas within the text and the page numbers where they can be found.

### Glossary

Located at the back of the book, the glossary defines key words and phrases that are related to the topic. These words and phrases can be found in the text in colored type.

### Index

Located at the back of the book, an index is an alphabetical list of topics and the page numbers where they can be found.

With a little help and guidance about reading nonfiction, you can feel good about introducing a young reader to the world of *Little Mitchie* nonfiction books.

Little Mitchie is an imprint of:

Mitchell Lane
PUBLISHERS

2001 SW 31st Avenue
Hallandale, FL 33009
mitchelllanepub.com



First Edition, 2027.

Author: Kim Thompson
Designer: Bobbie Houser

Library of Congress Cataloging-in-Publication Data
Title: It Tastes Yucky / by Kim Thompson

Description: Hallandale, FL :
Mitchell Lane Publishers, [2027]

Identifiers:
ISBN 979-8-89260-859-6 (library bound)
ISBN 979-8-89260-956-2 (eBook)

Library of Congress Control Number: 2026935747

PHOTO CREDITS
Shutterstock: Ton Ponchai, cover, 1, 3, 4, 6, 12, 20; polkadot_photo, 5; New Africa, 7; PeopleImages, 8, 14; Diedov Denys, 10; Iamhaeruman, 13; 9foto, 17; languste, 18; Utikhrt, 18; bykot photo, 18; Pixel-Shot, 19; Maridav, 21; silamime, 22.

# TABLE OF CONTENTS

## Chapter One

# YUCK!

You lick cranberry sauce from a spoon at Thanksgiving. Yuck!

Your hot dog is covered in sauerkraut. Yuck!

You sip old milk from the back of the fridge. Double yuck!

Different people like different foods. A flavor that is unpleasant to you may be someone else's favorite. Everyone agrees, though, about spoiled, rotten, or **toxic** substances. They definitely taste awful.

Chapter Two

# THE SCIENCE OF TASTE

Your tongue is covered in bumps called **papillae**. These are not taste buds. Taste buds are structures inside papillae.

Tiny hairs called microvilli stick out of taste buds. They sense chemicals in your food. They send **signals** to your brain. That's how you know if you are tasting something delicious or gross.

Taste buds detect five flavors. They are sweet, sour, salty, bitter, and savory.

Kids have thousands more taste buds than adults. To young people, strong flavors taste even stronger. This may be why many kids dislike sour or bitter foods.

TASTY TIDBIT

It is untrue that different sections of your tongue taste different flavors. All five flavors are sensed all over your tongue.

Your tongue and nose are tasting partners. As you chew, food smells go up your nose. Sense **receptors** get triggered. Your brain gets more information about the flavor of your food.

Chapter Three

# YUCKY TASTES?

Sour flavors are sharp and tangy. They come from **acids** in foods. People **ferment** some foods to make them acidic and sour. For example, yogurt is fermented milk.

Some people think sour flavors are yucky. How do you feel about these sour foods?

- cranberries
- grapefruit
- kimchi
- lemons
- pickles
- plain yogurt
- sauerkraut
- sour candy
- sour cherries
- sour cream
- tomatoes
- vinegar

**TASTY TIDBIT**

When you taste something sour, your face may scrunch up. Your lips may pucker.

Bitter flavors are sharp and **pungent**. They come from chemicals in foods such as phenols, flavonoids, and caffeine.

Some people think bitter flavors are yucky. How do you feel about these bitter foods?

- artichokes
- broccoli
- brussels sprouts
- coffee
- dark chocolate
- dill
- eggplant
- ginger
- green tea
- kale
- mint
- the white part of an orange or lemon peel

**TASTY TIDBIT**

Bitter flavors taste different to different people. Some people are sensitive to bitter flavors. Some people can't taste them at all.

An **aversion** to strong flavors helps people survive. Extremely sour foods are probably not safe to eat. Spoiled milk is very sour. It contains harmful **bacteria**. The bacteria change sugar in the milk into lactic acid.

Flavors that are very bitter can be a warning. They signal that something is toxic. Many poisonous plants are bitter.

## TASTY TIDBIT

Spoiled and rotten food may have **mold** growing on it. Eating it can make you sick.

Chapter Four

# YUCK TO YUM

As you get older, you visit new places. You meet new people. You get introduced to different foods.

Don’t be afraid to try a little bite. You could be pleasantly surprised! You might even change your mind about something you thought was yucky.

# WINNER DINNER

**Ingredients:**

A base food that everyone likes, such as macaroni and cheese, mashed potatoes, or hot dog chunks

Five toppings that have sour or bitter flavors, such as pickles, sour cream, chopped tomatoes, sauerkraut, broccoli, brussels sprouts, chopped kale, or fresh dill

A prize, such as a dessert, an extra hour of screen time, or a special activity

**Directions:**

1. For each person, prepare five small servings of the base food.
2. Put the toppings in bowls and set them in the center of the table.
3. Challenge each person to sample five different toppings on their food.
4. As you eat, observe and discuss. Did anyone pucker their lips or make a face? Did anyone discover a new flavor they liked?
5. Award the prize to brave eaters who tasted five different flavors!

# GLOSSARY

**acids (AS-ids)** chemicals that contain hydrogen ions, usually dissolve in water, have a sour taste, and have a pH less than seven

**aversion (uh-VUHR-zhuhn)** a desire to turn away from something or avoid it

**bacteria (bak-TEER-ee-uh)** microscopic, single-celled living things

**ferment (fur-MENT)** to use bacteria or yeast to break down the chemicals in a substance

**mold (mohld)** a kind of fungus that grows on old food or on things that are warm and moist

**papillae (puh-PILL-ee)** small bumps on the tongue that contain taste buds

**pungent (PUHN-juhnt)** having a strong, sharp taste or smell

**receptors (ri-SEP-turz)** nerve endings that are sensitive to stimuli in the environment such as smells

**signals (SIG-nuhlz)** chemical and electrical messages that get sent to the brain through the body's nervous system

**toxic (TAHK-sik)** poisonous

# FURTHER READING

Highlights. *The Ultimate Science Cookbook for Kids: A Cookbook for Young Scientists That Transforms the Kitchen into a Food Lab for Learning.* Highlights Press, 2025.

Howl, Vanessa. *The Foodie Flamingo.* Running Press Kids, 2021.

# ON THE INTERNET

**SciShow: What Happens When Food Goes Bad?**
*youtube.com/watch?v=8n3guja-ukg*
Find out what happens when food rots and spoils.

**The Lean Green Bean: 75 New Foods to Try at Home**
*theleangreenbean.com/new-foods-to-try*
Find a list of 75 foods that might become your new favorites!

# INDEX